CW01560926

hedgerow #149

a journal of small poems

edited by Caroline Skanne

ISBN: 9798293729579

published by:
wildflower poetry press

www.wildflowerpoetrypress.com

hedgerowhaiku.com

cover photograph & design: Caroline Skanne
editor: Caroline Skanne

hedgerow is a short-poetry journal dedicated to publishing an eclectic mix of new and established voices across the spectrum of the short poem, with particular attention to English-language haiku & related works.

Submission reminders are emailed out ahead of each issue. If you are not currently on the mailing list, simply send an email with the subject heading 'subscribe' to:

hedgerowsubmission@gmail.com

just enough
to know they're out there
            frog songs

under the spell
of her fiddle
moonshine

Ben Gaa

a longing to visit
my ancestors' graves
first lilacs

storm clouds—
the pale filaments
of a sunlit willow

Jennifer Burd

more sign than symptom hard summer rain

blackbird   honeymoon

Cherie Hunter Day

intermittent rain
all of us singing loudly
out of tune

Jamie Wimberly

the day it changed snowdrops

th. vandergrau

even when
we don't deserve it—
white trillium

long winter night
another passage
into the fort

Lisa Gerlits

a prayer card with the wreath open sea

sunspot
no dog
to fill it

the space
where his tent stood
early dark

frances angela

buffalo skull
the braided smoke
of sweetgrass and sage

a break in the clouds—
the books I keep within
easy reach

Chad Lee Robinson

another page
of wildflowers
morning light

Joanna Ashwell

choosing to follow
a desire path
the smell of summer

Gareth Nurden

a day immersed
in the cuckoo's song
swaying bog cotton

graveside visit
on leaving we notice
the speedwell

a bugle's flowers
in woodland shade
the weir already a trickle

Thomas Powell

swift current
a dipper dives
into its song

Debbie Strange

April
still
deciding

Julie Schwerin

purple scorpion-weed
sprouts in the dry creekbed—
my first lucid dream

her ashes outdoors,
the urn on the mantel
now filled with flowers

Rebecca Lilly

early spring morning:
workmen hack the ice rink
back into a pond

Maeve O'Sullivan

mild day . . .
the dandelion seedhead
unblown

Frank Williams

spring gusts
a pair of puffins
line their burrow with grass

an ancient coral's
trace in stone . . .
sea thrift in bloom

after rain—
the river thundering
over rocks we stood on

Hannah Mahoney

steep mountain road . . .
the radio turns
to static

Jacob D. Salzer

a room above a railway
the rumble of the first train
through a drizzling dawn

Howard Colyer

late winter
the wet smell
of delivery boxes

dawn moon
cutting scone dough
into eighths

Brad Bennett

a bracing westerly—
autumn leaves fly
through the boat basin

Peter Barnes

spring morning
the up and down lines
gleam into the distance

honeysuckle
the uncut meadow
silvered by rain

John Barlow

payals clink
gathering wet clothes
the smell of earth

Jiel Narvekar

river reeds
from their quiet
a warbler's voice

Colin Oliver

also awake
in the small hours the mouse
nesting in the wall

Beverly Acuff Momoi

her engine's hum
coming up the hill
october dusk

John Pappas

warm wind
a wisp of horsehair
caught on the cholla

Dyana Basist

payday
mackerel skies
all that's left

Matthew Caretti

windy shore
the touch
of a feather

Pat Davis

I start
singing too
spring sunrise

Bryan Rickert

petals drifting . . .
the baby's room
still empty

Marion Alice Poirier

morning light a squirrel's tail full of autumn

Frank Hooven

first draft leaf shadows skim the page

waterlily bud unfolding first quarter moon

Kathryn Liebowitz

Still life

High above the forest, dawn blooms in a poppy. Here on the duff, I do my best to look dead.

    shadowlands
    rouging my forehead
    with borrowed blood

Sara Tropper

the afterglow
of summer sunset
I'm alone
at the margin
of this city noise

Chen-ou Liu

i have maps now
in the autumn
and lose time
i can't afford
to lose

i break
the silence
by sipping
what's left
of hot tea

ai li

driving from
store to store
to find the right
dark suit . . .
white lilies

Nicholas Gentile

The hour too late
for a country bus
—moonlight and
the long road.

Tim Chamberlain

one bowl
of rice
the steam

ai li

peace rose
your simple
casket

Sharon Rhutasel Jones

always something
there to remind me
autumn wind

Rick Tarquinio

gunshots
a skein of geese
fly into the sun

Joseph P. Wechselberger

world war two map
over the blackboard
won't roll back up

Randy Brooks

homesick
pressed against the picture window
a split leaf monstera

Anne Burgevin

not sticking
to the set list—
on and off rain

Laurie D. Morrissey

toys in the attic
from the dusty music box
a Schubert lullaby

Sylvia Forges-Ryan

blue sky
across the meadow
dandelion puffs

Katie Montagna

flower moon bookmarking the dogwood

Marilyn Ashbaugh

a trampled rose
on the sidewalk—
spring darkness

Maurizio Brancaleoni

I wake to birdsong—
the morning
you are gone

Tony Williams

cherry in blossom
the cuckoo's
first note

Karen Robbie

freewheeling
down the *bóithrín*
summer stillness

Audrey Quinn

a wasp
slips through a slit in the screen
slow afternoon

river rocks keeping the ones mother found

Ruth Holzer

whether it stops or not — snowfall

Victor Ortiz

the mating trill
of grasshopper sparrows
tornado debris

Eric Sundquist

three generations'
love of butterflies—
the finished quilt

Joan D. Stamm

sunflowers . . .
paintbrush soaked
in linseed oil

Kila Lim

spring rain
a woman eats an orange
in St Luke's graveyard

Chris Hardy

a snail raises its eyes
and nothing else
feels like rain

Peter Yovu

descending
         dusk
             barn owl

Ralph Stott

empty signboard,
empty parking lot . . .
autumn leaves

Marshall Bood

after the news
steaming the label
from a tin

C.X. Turner

all night rain—
the flume
of broken gutters

Judson Evans

icing my foot I sign the tax return

Robert Epstein

dusk
the blue of bluebells
beginning to blur

Erica Ison

snowflakes on my eyelashes
counting the reasons
to stick around

Kelly Sargent

forcing a needle
into the pinhole camera . . .
winter light

Richard Tindall

still water
the evening star
through her fingers

lit windows
from the wood's edge
an unfamiliar song

Evan Vandermeer

tracing the ravine's edge coyote call

Kathryn P. Haydon

losing my bearings
the labyrinth
of hospital corridors

Cynthia Anderson

the scent of my homeland in a lemon

Fatma Zohra Habis

wind ripples
through wattle blossoms
whistling honeyeaters

Louise Hopewell

a cloud moves on
the forsythia changed
and unchanged

Laszlo Slomovits

outside
of sunlight
a daisy chain

spring approaching—
distant
gunfire

John Gonzalez

through the hole
in Mên-an-Tol
the wren's song

Mark Rutter

turning back
turning over the shell
turned over by the sea

Gary Hotham

sea breeze
hollyhocks taller
than the abandoned skiff

Paula Sears

out of the fog
swans low over the sea
into the fog

Christer Hansson

the old cat
seeks out sunshine
counting days

Heather Lurie

spring evening
from my daughter's room
a fairy tale for the dolls

Irena Iris Szewczyk

new country
the familiarity
of unfamiliar birds

Helen Ogden

prairie twilight
slipping out of thought
into stillness

Mike Stinson

brittle cattails
a red-winged blackbird
scattering seeds

Mark Forrester

night sky
a prayer for you
left unsaid

Christine Eales

the rubber band on my address book stretched thin   another condolence card

Leslie Umans

blue moon
through wind-blown spruce boughs
the flicker of bats

stream crossing the songburst of a purple finch

Kristen Lindquist

you cancel
yet again
stargazing

if I recall correctly unicorns

Tim Gardiner

late summer becoming a husk

Joshua St. Claire

Printed in Dunstable, United Kingdom